Beyond the Mailbox

Annette Sprouls Reasoner

Beyond the Mailbox. Copyright 2017 by Annette Sprouls Reasoner. All rights reserved. No part of this book may be used or reproduced in any manner whatsoever without written permission.

Cover design by Merry Fuhrer 2017

ISBN-13: 978-0692968390

ISBN-10: 0692968393

Introduction

Mailboxes are filled with messages from the outside world, but sometimes that is as close as the outside world comes to a person's home. They are filled with reminders that bills are due, friends seldom write, and there are a million new products or services supposedly essential to our survival. Mailboxes are filled, but sometimes the spaces behind the mailboxes remain filled with loneliness, pain, and sadness not noticed by the outside world.

The mail carrier delivers to the mailbox, but beyond that mailbox often lies someone whose only contact with the outside world is that mail carrier. A choice is made. Deliver to the mailbox, move to the next, finish, go home. The other choice is to deliver to the person who lives beyond the mailbox, acknowledge the life, listen to the stories, and realize that we have much more to offer to each other than the daily barrage of bills and advertisements.

I listened to the stories. Some were spoken, some observed, some were read between unspoken lines. As I listened, my life story began to change. I had always been uneasy around people, most often walking with my head down, to avoid eye contact. When I began lifting my eyes to see the lives around me, my life changed. Interactions began adding to my story. Some people added words, some added sentences, paragraphs, even entire chapters that have become part of my story. I hope I added something to their stories, and I hope that the reader will take from these stories a willingness to look beyond the superficial to see the person, acknowledge the things so often overlooked, and listen to the stories.

The Bicycle Lady

I spoke to her yesterday for the first time, though I have lived here 23 years.

I don't know where she worked, but she rode her bicycle out of our small town each morning, back each evening, always wearing a dress and a fancy hat. I worked in the neighboring town and my commute by car was 18 minutes. I once saw her returning home, balancing two 2x4 pieces of lumber on her bike, probably to be used to repair her home which sat by itself on a road occupied only by her and an empty warehouse.

She does not ride her bicycle anymore. She pushes it, her constant companion. Perhaps she cannot ride anymore. Perhaps it serves to keep her from falling. Perhaps the handlebars are useful places on which to hang her items. These are, I learned, all partial truths.

I am guilty. She likes living alone. She likes to be independent. She doesn't want to be bothered. She is just eccentric. She will be fine. All the things we think about other people so that we somehow excuse ourselves from having to care; all the narratives we conjure to avoid having to look at an individual, to avoid having to see with compassion; of all these things, I stand guilty.

On my evening walk, I saw a bicycle propped against the stands at the Little League ballpark. The tires were almost completely bare. She sat on a bench in the shade but arose quickly as I approached. I greeted her and noticed immediately her calming presence and eyes that spoke of grace both given and received. She had been to Wednesday evening church services, she said, but no one else showed up. I offered her a ride home, it was hot outside, but she declined. I walked the remaining two blocks to my home. I was disappointed in myself. Why had I not done more, said more? She had missed church services; perhaps we could have held "church" in the shade of the baseball stands.

But perhaps, we had done just that.

Lillian

I do not know how long she had lived alone. Whether she was widowed or divorced I did not know. I did know there were three steps up to the front door, steps that she could not use. There was also a ramp, and a mailbox placed lower than most so it could be accessed from her wheelchair. I knew that her right leg was gone, but I did not know for how long it had been gone. I knew she had worked for years as a cook. I knew she was lonely. She told me that all her friends had died. She joked that they must all be sitting together in heaven shaking their heads, saying, "Poor Lillian, she didn't make it up here."

She was always waiting for me when I delivered her mail. We talked, and though at the time my feet were aching from heel spurs, I stood and listened, not daring to complain. At least I had two feet. She spoke often of her phantom pain, a pain coming from the leg that was no longer there. It kept her up many nights she said, and I could see that the pain was indeed intense. Phantom pain was an unfamiliar term to me. Pain that originates from a place that no longer exists seemed impossible. I never doubted her though.

Aside from this pain, she was very healthy and more than capable of taking care of herself. Never had to go to the doctor, she said, never sick. So when she contracted pneumonia that winter, her children panicked. "Mother never gets sick. She won't be able to take care of herself. She can't live here alone." So, they moved her out. It made her angry, and rightfully so, because home was now a small room in a nursing facility, shared with a total stranger. Once a professional cook, she now found herself at the mercy of the kitchen staff, and she despised that food. Her large house she lived in alone must have seemed so full; the new residence swallowed up by two beds, two chairs, two televisions and two people must have seemed so empty.

I think of her often. I think of the fullness of her life and the emptiness of her life. I think also of phantom pain in a broader sense. I think of pain that comes from empty spaces and arises from voids in our lives. I think of my family's loss. An empty chair at the kitchen table. An empty spot on the sofa. My father used to sit there. He once saw me take my first steps in this world. I saw him take his last, and my legs became crippled. How would I navigate through life? Like Lillian, a part of me had been taken away, and the pain of that void would resonate forever. Like her, I would adjust and adapt, but the pain of the empty spaces would always be present. Like her, I awoke one day to find the confines of my life had become smaller while the emptiness became larger.

Lillian's grandson and his new wife moved immediately into the house, and I wondered, as two new sets of feet now greeted the floor of this house each morning, if phantom pain arose from what used to exist between these walls. I wondered if what had been taken away ever crossed their minds.

There were three steps up to the front door. A ramp no longer needed. A mailbox lower than most. And a house that bore witness to the pain of empty spaces.

Ducker

I visited Lillian in the nursing home a few times. She did have to share the tiny room with another person, so it was not easy, or polite, to leave her roommate out of the conversation. She introduced herself as June, and she and Lillian seemed to share the same wry sense of humor, and perhaps eased one another's loneliness. The second time I visited, I noticed June's last name on the door to the room. As we spoke, I studied her face.

In high school, we had a tradition that for some girls, myself included, could be a little humiliating. I suppose every school has some tradition or ritual that, whether intended or not, excludes or singles out certain individuals. Valentine's Day was my day of dread. Under the guise of a fundraiser, boys would buy roses for their girlfriends, which would then be delivered during homeroom period. Some girls received so many that it was suspected their fathers had padded the numbers a bit. I never received a rose, never expected to receive a rose, and everyone knew I would not receive a rose. So, in my senior year, when my name was called, I felt every eye was on me as I made my way to the front of the class to take my rose. I placed it on my desk and stared at it, afraid to read the attached card. Surely someone must be playing a joke on me. Finally, I snuck a peek. The card had but one name on it: Ducker. I held out hope all day that somewhere in that school was a boy whose last name or nickname was Ducker, but in reality, I knew the truth. I never said a word about that rose.

So as I sat in Lillian's room, studying June's face, I knew time had given me a second chance. The name on the door had been Ducker. June Ducker, the school nurse from my high school, now lived in a nursing home. She remembered me. I had worked in her office my senior year. She remembered my brother. She remembered the rose. I am sure she remembered that I had never acknowledged her gift to the awkward teenager whom she knew would not get a rose otherwise, but that she did not mention. Now, decades later, I was given another gift, the gift of being able to thank her for the gesture that meant more than she ever knew.

Odessa

She kept everything that entered her physical world. Her car was evidence enough of that. Only the driver's seat remained visible, surrounded by the stacks of magazines, newspapers, coffee cups, food wrappers and no doubt several inches of the junk mail I delivered to her each day. The remnants of everyday life filled her spaces, with only enough room remaining for her and her Chihuahua.

Summertime kept her occupied tending the garden, which oddly enough was very neat and trim. Winter came, and she sat each day in the car, engine running, Chihuahua perched atop the clutter in the passenger seat. She read. The dog slept. Initially I thought that the heat in her house had been shut off and she was sitting in the car to stay warm. This was not the case. This was just her way.

She stored up words like she stored up possessions, and when she spoke to me it was as if the floodgates of her mind had burst open. This was a problem, because she lived near the end of my mail route, and if I weren't already behind schedule, I soon would be. Her conversations were like her car, allowing only room for herself. I could not have pushed one word through the corridor of her sentences. So, I listened. And I fell behind. I liked her. She had a keen sense of humor and was very intelligent, but Christmas was nearing, my workload was expanding and daylight hours were diminishing. Time constraints, either real or imagined, led me to more often duck my head when passing, hoping to not be noticed.

She died on Christmas Day. Her family lived nearby, but they found her body two days later. I was shocked at their lack of grief, but not at my sense of guilt and lost opportunities. Her son-in-law delivered the news to me. He was a preacher. He would do the service, he said, but he was NOT going to clean up THAT MESS! He pointed at the house, as full as her car, only enough space carved out for her and her Chihuahua. But who had carved out enough space in their lives for her?

She kept everything that entered her physical world, things most of us would throw away. Now her belongings have been discarded, and a Chihuahua remains. Her daughter moved into the house several months later. She sat often in her mother's car, parked in the driveway, a Chihuahua in the passenger seat; a testament perhaps to what had been shared and what had been lost.

Abraham

Invariably he would wait until I was across the street. Then his screams would begin. Trying to call me back, incessantly he yelled, "excuse me!" Tired and almost finished for the day, I tried to ignore him, but he would not stop. I went back. All he wanted, I learned, was the mail, but he could not reach the mailbox. He was only 5, already overweight and his clothing of choice was a t-shirt, only a t-shirt, nothing else.

It was weeks before I discovered the real reason for his shouts. His grandmother was alone inside, legally blind, an amputee confined to a wheelchair. Oh, she could get the mail herself, she explained, but this was the one thing he felt he could do to help her. But he could not do it alone, so he stood as we all sometimes do, in his helplessness and nakedness, screaming "excuse me!" to a world that tries not to notice.

The house burned last month. Yellow caution tape now stretches around the corpse of a home, plywood fills the window frames and a single bright blue toy rests on the porch. I knew she had passed away five years prior.

Abraham would be an adult now. I had not known her husband, but heard that neighbors would often leave bags of food hanging on the door for him; bags that sometimes stayed for days untouched, just like the letters in the mailbox. I also learned he had recently moved out, homeless people had moved in and the fire ultimately claimed the space for itself.

I drive by the house often and think of Abraham shouting from the porch. Now this house stands alone in its nakedness, the memories once made and shared within its walls perhaps crying out from the ashes to be noticed, "excuse me!"

The Yellow House

If the old metal bench outside the old social security office is empty, I know I will find him across the parking lot, under a shade tree at the Burger King, drinking from a McDonald's coffee cup.

He had introduced himself to me when I first took over this route. I remember his name, fairly certain he does not remember mine, and our conversations consist mostly of his asking me three or four times, "How you been?" First, however, he offers a handshake and a smile.

On wintry days, he may be found sitting inside the almost abandoned office building, on the one chair at the one table upon which rests a copy of the King James Bible. Other days may be cold enough to bring him inside the McDonald's, where he uses his gift card to purchase a cup of coffee, sit and enjoy endless refills. He occasionally offers to buy a cup for me. I decline, although certain that he would appreciate the opportunity to share something, anything. He does not realize that his friendliness is a gift he shares with me each day. I give him bottled water in the summer. He does not decline, but accepts with a smile and his repetitious greeting.

I never ask if he is homeless. He does not carry belongings, other than his Styrofoam coffee cup, with him. Once he told me that he lives in a big yellow house with green grass and beautiful flowers everywhere. The street name he gave was over 5 miles away from his bench, well off the bus route. Real or imagined, a large yellow house surrounded by flowers and the greenest grass sounded a bit like heaven, and I am certain there is room enough there for him.

Just Move

I knew that the elderly couple's only son had recently passed away. I rarely saw the woman. The man I saw often, and he was always very talkative and pleasant. Pleasant, that is, until the conversation turned to his wife. He hated her, he said; all she ever does is sit in her room and cry. He had moved past his grief. She had not, and for that reason he hated her. He called her horrible names. I wondered how long it had been since their relationship had been marked by love. I wondered if this animosity was a new thing, or if perhaps her now deceased son had been the only one who loved her in return.

I saw her finally one spring day. She remarked with great excitement how beautiful her flowers were (they were weeds). She was cleaning the yard, and had filled a large trash can. I offered to dump it for her. She said NO! in such a loud voice that I stepped back quickly. She was adamant, explaining that she had to do it herself. She needed to do it herself. For months she had stayed in bed, overcome with such grief that she could not even raise her arms. Now she had to move. She needed to move. It was important. She needed to move past the crippling grief. And I then saw not a helpless elderly woman despised by her husband. I saw a strong woman coming back to life.

And her flowers were beautiful.

Herman

He lived east of town in a trailer with his four dogs. Each day he rode his bicycle about a mile to the only store in the area, a place where local farmers gathered to drink coffee and talk. They all welcomed Herman to their table. Herman had no teeth. He ate ice cream in the summer, soup in the winter. And he drank coffee with his friends. When the weather turned harsh, someone would put the bike in the back of a pickup and drive Herman home. When his daily trip required the purchase of a large bag of dog food, someone would put the bag and the bike in the back of a pickup and drive Herman home.

His trailer was small. He had replaced the front door with a blanket so the dogs could come and go as they pleased.

One winter day found wind chill readings dip well below zero. Herman died that day in his trailer, surrounded by four dogs. None of us had thought to check on him. None of us knew that the four dogs were his only source of heat.

We later learned that he had family in town. They said he had always refused their help. We had offered him help, but not when it really mattered. We failed him. We always stopped short, driving him to the home with no door, never bothering to venture further.

Henry

The house was already small but had become tiny for the man who found himself confined to a hospital bed in the front room. For him, the house had become one room. A portable toilet was stationed between the bed and the front door. It was summer, and a single fan and an open screen door were the only things cooling the room; a single fan, blowing past the toilet toward the screen door and across the porch where the mailbox was positioned.

He had worked for the Post Office in his younger days. I delivered his mail now, and he always wanted to talk. But sometimes – most times – the stench was overbearing, and I tried to slip by unnoticed.

His wife had become ill and had to be placed in a rehab facility. Left without a caretaker, he had to be removed from his small house and tiny room, which must have seemed a mansion compared to his new bed in the nursing home. He had hoped to return whenever his wife was able to do so, but the house was condemned by the city, deemed uninhabitable. He once told me that he had paid $8,000 for that house, brand new. Now it is gone, demolished, occupying no physical space. So is Henry.

A person first occupies the world, then a house, then a room, then a hospital bed. A shrinking life is this, marked by events or people who often treat others as the city treats an old house.

And I tried to slip by unnoticed.

The Sidewalk

She was very tall, even stooped over, shoulders slumped, head hung low. She always walked in this manner, a slow easy gait, hands clasped behind her back, staring only at the sidewalk.

I had seen her on my route many times. Co-workers had seen her too, many blocks away. Some of my customers were afraid of her, or suspicious. They questioned me about her. They avoided her. One woman closed her door when she saw her.

One day as I passed, I spoke. Only "Hello." But her head lifted and in an awkward, much too loud voice that must have surprised her as much as it did me, she answered. Only "Hello." Our eyes met for a moment, then her gaze fell back down and we continued walking. Perhaps for a moment her world had become more than just the sidewalk at which she stared. I know mine had.

Tanya

Two cars travelling in the same direction.

Two lives taking different paths.

It was a rear-end collision of such force that her car was launched a full city block from point of impact. His car continued in the opposite direction, striking the vehicle of the sole witness to the early morning crash. This was the trajectory of their cars, each detail mapped out in spray paint on the pavement, a complicated maze difficult to decipher, difficult to comprehend.

The trajectory of their lives was that she died.

She drove for Uber, working nights providing rides to those who had too much to drink. He had too much to drink that night; a pocketful of bar receipts told the story of his evening. Fifteen minutes after paying for his last drink, their paths crossed, but not through the Uber app.

The irony of her being killed by a drunk driver was obvious, but a deeper irony took shape as I studied the accident scene. The spray-painted lines that indicated a death had occurred went over the curb and covered the newly emerging blades of green grass. Signs of death and new life together in one spot, this spot that was the final resting place of her car.

Doug

He met me on the driveway. He was pacing, nervous, waiting for the arrival of the veterinarian, who was to administer the injection that would end the suffering of his feline companion.

"Do you want to see her?" His cat, did I want to see his cat?

I did not know what was expected of me. Did he want verification from me that he had made the correct decision? Was my seeing the cat really so important to him, or was he simply trying to fill the empty time? I agreed, entered the house and was led to the room where his cat rested on the white leather couch. He told me the cat's name, but I remember neither that nor what I whispered into the cat's fur. I do remember the stillness of the room, the tears in Doug's eyes as I stood, and the quiet thank you he offered.

I had grieved with him months before over the death of his wife, his wife who adored that cat. Now he invited me to grieve with him again, and I was grateful to have been able to experience a sacred moment in the midst of an ordinary workday.

Red Ants

Their yard, their sidewalk, their driveway…all covered with red ants. There were so many in fact that I had to make my way as quickly as possible to the mailbox on the porch, then to the street to avoid the sidewalk swarm.

He met me at the door one day. A double amputee, confined to a wheelchair, living in a house with no outside ramp, he had but one simple request. He asked me to lower the mailbox so he could open the door, reach inside the box and get the mail. I agreed. There were already nails in place, so I guessed the mailbox used to be there anyway.

A few days later, the mailbox was moved again, this time placed on the yard's chain link fence, next to the driveway. Easier for me, I didn't have to walk so far. I guessed that his granddaughter who lived there had moved it so he could not get the mail. I was right.

One day I saw him outside the house. On his stomach he crawled through the carpet of red ants, using his elbows to propel himself. He reached the mailbox and struggled to get the mail that could not have been of any real importance to him. Certainly it could have waited until someone else came home. But his was a struggle for so much more.

Joyce

She carried with her the anger of not being allowed to die.

In her younger years she had died, but was brought back to life. Her voice was full of joy, tranquility, as she spoke of the place she had briefly visited after having left this world. Her voice then turned to anger, rage, as she related how furious she was that the doctors had brought her back to this place. She wanted to stay there!

She had made the most of the situation, I suppose. She had been married over 60 years. She had a rescue dog, which, ironically, she had saved from death, and which put the same joy in her eyes as did memories of the afterlife she had visited so many years ago. So she did not spend her days in despair, nor did she seem inclined to hasten her departure from this earth. But her anger rose to the surface often, especially as she aged and her health declined.

I visited the neighborhood a couple years ago. I had not seen Joyce for several years, and did not initially recognize the woman in the wheelchair accompanied by a home health care worker. I crossed the street to say hello, but the vacant eyes and blank expression told me that not only would she not remember me, but also that she really had, in a sense, already departed this world. She passed away shortly thereafter, and I wonder often about the place she inhabited briefly so many years ago, and hope that it was all she had remembered.

Katy

She met me on the porch, wearing her mother's heels, jewelry and a blouse that swallowed her twelve-year-old frame. The story hiding behind this simple game of dress-up was that Katy's mother had been dead for three years. She and her father had recently moved into a house on my route, and I recognized them from church and knew their story. I secretly hoped they did not remember me.

It should not have mattered. I am ashamed that I allowed it to matter. The family began attending the church when Katy was eight. Katy's mother took pictures constantly during church service. She photographed everything: her daughter as an acolyte, her daughter reading the liturgy, her daughter in the children's choir, the children's pageant. This was prior to the introduction of the smartphone, which provided a world of distractions at one's fingertips. This was prior to the digital camera. This was flash photography, standing up and moving around during the service to get the perfect shot. It should not have mattered. But I mumbled. It was distracting. It was disrespectful. At the time, that church did not even allow flash photography during wedding ceremonies in the sanctuary. It was a different time. But it still should not have mattered to me.

I later learned that the mother had been diagnosed with advanced breast cancer. She knew she was not going to live. She wanted her family to attend church together. She took pictures to preserve memories. She enjoyed her time with her family. That mattered.

They did not remember me. We became acquainted and I watched her father struggle to raise a daughter by himself. I watched Katy grow up and make college plans. Last year, Katy and her father moved to Florida to start a new life. She arrived home one day to find him unresponsive. He had fallen in the bathroom, and sustained a brain injury. His parents and brothers drove in from Texas to be by his side as he was removed from life support.

Katy had nine years with her mother, twenty-one years with her father. Not much time to make memories. I think of the photographs her mother took, the memories she tried to preserve. They did matter.

Ringer

I found her on 9/11. There were no planes flying that evening, and the air was heavy with silent despair and shock. I sat in the grass in the backyard, trying to escape the horrifying images on television. The stray cat I had been feeding ate then quickly disappeared over the fence. I knew she had been pregnant but no longer was, and I had wondered where she was keeping her kittens. I found them just beyond my fence in the neighbor's junk pile, well hidden.

There was something wrong with one of the kittens. She was perhaps ten days old, eyes just opening, aware of her surroundings but unaware of the fact that early in her life she had crawled partially through a small PVC pipe fitting that had remained around her midsection while she grew larger. The ring around her belly was now so tight that she certainly could not have lived much longer.

So in the midst of the suffocating fear, dread, grief and hopelessness that had wrapped itself so tightly around the nation, we were able to free this kitten. The mother, so cautious around us, waited outside the back door while we meticulously pried the plastic apart. The mother and kitten eventually became our housecats. We named the kitten Ringer. Each year as I remember the horror of that day's events, I also recall the story of Ringer and the few minutes that the air was heavy not with despair but with hope.

Jim

"Do you want to see my dead wife?"

Thankfully, he did not wait for an answer. A neighbor had informed me that the woman had passed away the day before. I had never met her, though I knew she had been ill for several months, and I had planned to knock on his door to offer my condolences. He was waiting on the porch. "Do you want to see my dead wife?" He swung both front doors open before I could answer. I cannot accurately enough describe my emotional state at that moment. I knew I was going to see something, and it was obvious I had no choice. It was a quick relief to see that prominently displayed on a table in the entryway was a very large, beautiful portrait of his wife, a portrait that initiated the first of many conversations between the two of us. We quickly became friends, and I checked on him each day as I delivered his mail. We talked on the porch a few minutes a day, not really solving the world's problems as much as merely identifying them. Jim's daughter told me that frequently she would be on the phone with her father, and he would hang up abruptly, because, as he said, the mail lady is here. He knew I would worry if he did not answer. Cali, his cat, always came out to greet me, rolling over for a belly scratch and obediently going back inside when it was time for me to leave. He always referred to Cali as "pretty good company."

He told me many times that he was ready to die. I promised to bake a cake for his 100th birthday, instead taking him to lunch on his 90th, which would turn out to be his last. For personal health reasons, I had to give up my mail route, and Jim died a few weeks later. I visited him in the hospital when he became ill. He asked only one thing of me. He made me promise that I would not allow anyone to "put down" his cat. I promised. During his stay in the hospital, I visited and fed Cali each day, until the family arrived. Cali no longer cared for me, and she certainly expressed a great dislike for the members of the family, as it was obviously our fault her friend was no longer at home. I eventually enlisted the help of friends to trap her and move her to my house, which was much smaller than hers and had to be shared with other cats. I gave her a small closet, which she occupied immediately, but she hated me. The same cat who greeted me each day now despised me. She blamed me. I blamed me. He told me for years he was ready to die. When our daily visits stopped, he died.

When my husband arrived home that evening, he had no idea we had a new resident. But when Cali heard his voice, she ran out of her closet and instantly they became friends. She greeted him each morning and each evening. She sat in his lap. She followed him around the house. She moved out of her closet. She adjusted. She tolerated me. We had her three years. She had a stroke. I kept my promise, though the vet told me she had little chance. Indeed, she did not last through that day, but waited for my husband to come home, and he sat on the floor with her and held her until the end. I had never seen him show such love and care for one of our pets. "Pretty good company" indeed.

Remember

I remember her house. The long room to the right of the front door, where there was a daybed and television. The long kitchen table full of relatives at the holidays.

I remember the small room at the center of the house, where the evaporative cooler blew the most wonderfully cool moist air right on my face.

I remember the aluminum chairs in the backyard. I still have one of them. I remember the short cinder block wall I liked to walk on.

I remember she often gave us Coke bottles, and we would carry them to the store down the block to collect the deposit money.

I remember when she had to be put in a nursing home. Her house was being cleaned out, and my uncle remarked that it felt like someone had died. "In a way, someone has," my father answered.

I remember finding out she had died. It was a summer morning and I was washing dishes. My father came in the kitchen, swallowed a glass of water, and with a voice I had never heard told me that Mom had died. He was crying. I had never heard him cry.

I remember crying in the bathroom, thinking that now my father was an orphan.

I remember her funeral. It was time for the family to go in, and my father stayed behind for a moment, his sobs echoing throughout the covered parking area. It was the second time I heard him cry.

I remember when my girl scout troop had gone to her nursing home to sing for the residents. Afterward, I persuaded my friend to go with me to my grandmother's room. She saw us, and began screaming for the staff to get these orphans out of her room.

She did not remember me.

And so I write about cold moist air blowing on my face, naps on a daybed, family meals at the long kitchen table, Coke bottles exchanged for coins which were exchanged for candy, tears witnessed and grief experienced because someday, I might not remember.

Blankets

The homeless sell newspapers on street corners each Sunday. Dropped off before dawn, picked up after dusk, they spend an entire day sometimes in rain or snow, freezing blustery northern winds, blistering 100° summer days, stinging springtime dust storms, or simply pleasant weekend weather that produces more traffic, more potential customers.

While stopped at a traffic light one Sunday, I found myself directly beside one of the vendors. My window was rolled down, we made eye contact, and his gaze shifted from me to the newspapers and back. "I don't have any money," I said. What I meant was that I did not have any cash; no paper money, no coins, nothing. He maintained eye contact. "Sure is a nice car you have", he said. "Those must cost a lot of money," he said. His voice had a mix of sarcasm and anger. The light changed to green, and as I drove away, the realization of his implication hit me. I told him I had no money, but I drove a "nice" car, so I must be a liar. It made me angry. I wanted to drive around the block again and explain to him that not everyone who has a car he deems to be "nice" has cash filling wallets, purses, gloveboxes, pockets. I wanted to explain that my car was almost ten years old and I was much too far in debt to ever afford another. I was angry.

Then another realization. He had made a blanket statement about me; he had seen me not as a person but as a stereotype. He had done to me what had probably been done to him the majority of his life. Blanket statements about the homeless abound and the statements that are thrown over them contain labels such as junkie, drunk, lazy, crazy, takers, fakers. They spend all their money on cigs and beer. They drive Cadillacs to the store and use food stamps. These are heavy blankets people use that enable them to avoid looking at the individual person, listening to the individual story. These are not the blankets that provide warmth.

I had a blanket statement thrown over me by a person who spent a lifetime hidden under them, a person who might own only one real blanket to provide warmth in a world that can prove to be very cold. I did not circle the block to confront him. His words had been harsh, but I left that intersection with a deeper understanding. Blankets can provide warmth and security, but when they are used to cover the truth, they can be as cold as the bitter north wind.

The Word of Choice

She wanted prayers for her son. He was dying. She had moved back to town to care for him, and now spoke with the preacher of her chosen denomination, asking if she could stand during service and request prayers for her son.

Yes, he said. Just don't tell them why.

Her son was dying of AIDS.

A longtime friend caught her after the service. The question came. What's wrong with your son? The answer came. The silence spoke volumes as her friend simply walked away. It was clear there were to be no prayers for her son.

In schools and playgrounds across the country, "fag" has always been the word of choice to humiliate, isolate and denigrate someone. In the spring of my ninth grade year, I watched in despair through the classroom window as the sky turned brown before lunchtime. The rolling clouds of dust common to our area arrived each day it seemed, bringing high winds that blew stinging dirt. This mattered to me because I could not eat lunch in the cafeteria. The word of choice had been attached to me, and it was made clear I was not welcome.

I retreated. The application of the word had not been accurate, but they did not concern themselves with facts. So I sat outside, hidden by the darkened sky, the dirt particles filling my hair and stinging my skin.

Now the silence stung the woman in the church. The word of choice had been attached to her son, and the clouds of dark despair must have seemed suffocating.

She found a new church that offered love and prayers. Schooldays passed, and I survived. But the word of choice remains a weapon in churches and schoolyards throughout the generations. And sometimes that weapon is lethal.

Number 5

Number 5 died last week. I started my new route two weeks before Christmas, and when I arrived at the eighteen-unit apartment complex the first time, two residents met me at the curb. Each unlocked his mailbox and stood glaring, arms crossed, saying not a word. They repeated this ritual every day. I called them Number 1 and Number 5. I tried to make conversation but was only informed that I was late, or that Number 1 was expecting his medicine from the VA, where was it? I offered them donuts and small talk, but received blank stares in return. So, I delivered the mail and they watched. Each day they walked in silence back to their respective apartments, and in silence I drove away.

It was a month before my attempts at conversation were successful. Number 5 began lingering at the mailbox, telling me the same stories every day. He had almost died twice, he said, suffering two heart attacks and triple bypass surgery. He had to quit his job as a truck driver, and his brother took care of his finances. He never wore a shirt, even in the winter. He never received any mail but current resident mail, so I did not know his name. He did not ask mine, I did not ask his. He was Number 5. Flowers grew outside his apartment door, but nowhere else on the property. I noticed often a bicycle parked outside his door, and recognized it as belonging to the mentally disabled man whom I had seen escorted out of several local restaurants. He was always welcome in Number 5.

The last time I saw Number 5, he told me he was on his way to visit another neighbor. It isn't good to sit in the house alone, he said, a person needs to have friends. It isn't living, being alone all day. Number 1 met me at the box the next day, informing me that I would not need to deliver number 5. He died. He had suffered a massive heart attack while visiting the afternoon before. He turned and walked away without waiting for his mail. It was weeks before I saw him again. The lady in number 9 announced in anger the next day that her friend had died. Neighbors asked me if I knew of any funeral arrangements. Everyone knew him as the man with no shirt. Everyone liked him. Everyone missed him. His life had not gone unnoticed. He had opened his doors and lived.

His name was Kenneth.

G.C.

I was not in the Christmas spirit. My truck was loaded with parcels on the busiest day of the season, and one package in particular fueled my anger. A signature was required for this package, and the house faced a busy seven lane thoroughfare. I would have to park on the nearest side street and walk to the house. It was cold. It was late. I was busy. I was angry. I knocked. A loud scream came from inside. I waited, identified myself, knocked again. Finally, he came to the door. I apologized for bothering him and explained that I needed his signature for the package. He asked me to come inside, took the form from me and struggled to write just his first and last initials.

"I have cancer. I want to die."

His words stung. I had never met this man. Maybe he was glad to be able to speak these words aloud to someone, anyone. Perhaps these were words he could not say to a family member, words they would not want to hear. Now, what words would I say to him? Years prior, after receiving the news of my father's terminal cancer, my sister and I were in the hospital elevator. Two strangers shared the elevator, and the woman spoke. "It looks like you girls got bad news," she said. "I want you to know our prayers are with you". She did not turn away from our grief. She acknowledged our pain and offered comfort. What words would I say to this man? I could only manage "I'm sorry."

My father and I never spoke of his illness. I prayed that he would be cured. Hope against hope, I prayed that he would be cured. Now this stranger's words echoed those of my own father as once I stood in the hallway outside his room and heard him pray to God, "please let me die, just please God let me die." His words stung. I knew this was a conversation I was not supposed to hear, but it was in that moment I realized that my prayers were not going to be answered. I stood now in this stranger's home, as he spoke aloud his wish, his "prayer." As I took the form from him, on which he had struggled to write his two initials, I noticed another form posted on his wall. His full signature lined the bottom of the form; the top had but three letters: DNR. Do Not Resuscitate. A prayer of sorts to please just let me die.

Twenty years prior I worked for a small company outside the city limits. A paramedic entered one day with a simple request. A witness was needed for the signing of a DNR. The woman lived in a trailer across the road. I did not know her, she did not know me, but I entered her home acting as witness to the signing of her wish, her prayer, to not be resuscitated. I did not speak to her, nor she to me. I should have said something. I wondered then if I might be interfering, overstepping. I wondered if there was a family that did not wish her to post that statement to please, just let me die. I was a witness to her signature, but not to her life. I cannot remember what she looked like. I do not know her name. I do not know for how much longer she lived. I should have said something.

I stood now with this man who signed his initials for the pain medicine I delivered, and witnessed so much more than two letters on a form, so much more than the three letters posted by the door. I helped him back to his chair. He screamed when he sat down. Bone cancer, then. I offered to get water so he could take his medication, but he declined. His daughter would be home soon. I looked around the room at the many paintings on the walls. His wife was an artist, he said. She died of cancer. He used to be an artist too, a woodworker. Those walls stick in my mind, walls that made it a home. A life is marked by the walls of a home. Wedding pictures are hung, then family portraits. Child's drawings cover refrigerator doors, cherished paintings and mementos fill the space. History is displayed on each wall, and everything is significant.

Then we hang a DNR. He died two weeks later.

Dottie

She no longer knows me.

Once her lifeline was marked by the usual peaks and valleys and level ground. Eventually that line became taut, pulled so by grief, despair and helplessness. Life began to pull her down and strangle her. Her husband forgot himself, forgot their love and spent his days dialing random phone numbers, in hopes of reaching any woman who could be convinced to abandon her life and run off with him. He lashed out at his wife, my friend. I saw the line pull tighter as she watched the man she loved slowly disappear, and she became entangled in emotional and physical exhaustion.

Her daughter lay in a nursing home 300 miles away, on life support, a victim of Multiple Sclerosis. Two children and a husband who did not love her kept the machine plugged in, and never visited. My friend made the trip to say goodbye to her daughter, who never heard the words and never saw her mother's face that day. There would be no peaks or valleys in her daughter's timeline anymore, but the line that marked Dottie's life wrapped itself around Dottie's hands, rendering her helpless to give her daughter the freedom and dignity she deserved. Her daughter did eventually die, and the husband gave her no funeral service.

I saw her timeline relax a bit when Dottie's husband passed away. Caring for him had drained her. By that time, he was confined to bed, unable to talk. She grieved, then found some peaks and some leveling in her life. There were valleys too. He had no life insurance. He had taken a reverse mortgage on the house without her knowledge. She became vulnerable, and fell victim to several scam artists. A petite woman who took pride in her appearance, she was courted by many widowers after her husband's death, but it was the man across the street who convinced her to marry again. He gathered her lifeline and shoved it into darkness. He cut her off from her friends. He fired the housecleaner and the yardman, who had been her companions for years. She always was dressed for a dinner date, even if she stayed at home, but he made her sell her clothes in a garage sale. Her weekly hair appointments were cancelled.

I saw her sitting in her driveway once and stopped to say hello. "Who is that?" she asked her new husband. It had only been a few months. Her lifeline was still there, but it held no memories. I knew her life like marks on an EKG readout, and I saw the moment her heart was forever changed and time held for her no memories, good or bad. I am grateful she does not remember the depths of the valleys she endured, yet give thanks that the good memories we shared have become forever a part of the peaks of my life.

I still know her.

www.ingramcontent.com/pod-product-compliance
Lightning Source LLC
Chambersburg PA
CBHW031436040426
42444CB00006B/843